S0-BIQ-364

SNAKES

Pit Vipers

by Adele D. Richardson

Consultants:

The staff of Black Hills Reptile Gardens

Rapid City, South Dakota

CAPSTONE
HIGH-INTEREST
BOOKS

an imprint of Capstone Press
Mankato, Minnesota

Capstone High-Interest Books are published by Capstone Press
151 Good Counsel Drive, P.O. Box 669, Mankato, Minnesota 56002
http://www.capstone-press.com

Library of Congress Cataloging-in-Publication Data
Richardson, Adele, 1966–
   Pit vipers / by Adele D. Richardson.
      p. cm.—(Snakes)
   Includes bibliographical references (p. 45) and index.
   Contents: Pit vipers—Pit viper species—Habitat—Hunting—Mating—Pit vipers
and people—Fast facts about pit vipers.
   ISBN 0-7368-2138-4
   1. Pit vipers—Juvenile literature. [1. Pit vipers. 2. Snakes. 3. Poisonous snakes.]
I. Title. II.Series: Snakes (Mankato, Minn.)
QL666.O69R52 2004
597.96'3—dc21   2003000460

Summary: Describes the physical features, habitat, and hunting and mating methods
of pit vipers, which include rattlesnakes, copperheads, cottonmouths, bushmasters, and
fer-de-lances.

Editorial Credits
Tom Adamson, editor; Patrick Dentinger, book designer; Jo Miller, photo researcher

Photo Credits
Cover: copperhead snake, Visuals Unlimited/Ann & Rob Simpson

Allen Blake Sheldon, 30
Bruce Coleman Inc./Gail M. Shumway, 12; Michael Fogden, 15, 24; Joe McDonald, 21
Corbis/Michael & Patricia Fogden, 32
Joe McDonald, 6, 18, 22, 36, 38, 41
Visuals Unlimited/Jim Merli, 8, 34; Rudolf Arndt, 10; Joe McDonald, 16–17, 27, 29;
   Ken Lucas, 44

1 2 3 4 5 6 08 07 06 05 04 03

Table of Contents

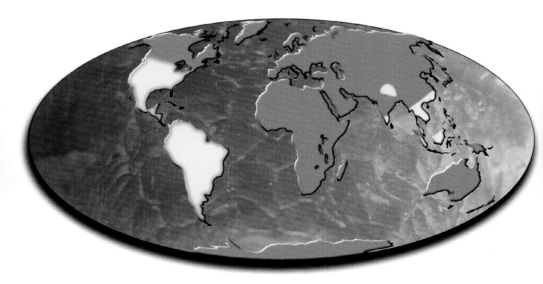

Yellow represents areas where pit vipers live.

Fast Facts about Pit Vipers

Scientific Names: Pit vipers are part of the Viperidae family. Pit vipers make up the subfamily called Crotalinae.

Size: Pit vipers grow to a variety of lengths. The hump-nosed pit viper can be as small as 1 foot (31 centimeters) long. The bushmaster can grow to more than 12 feet (3.7 meters) long.

Range: Pit vipers live in North America, Central America, South America, and Asia.

Description:	All pit vipers have hollow fangs that swing forward when the snakes are ready to strike. Pit vipers also have heat-sensing pits on their faces. The pits detect heat given off by an animal's body.
Habitat:	Pit vipers may live in deserts, forests, mountains, swamps, and grasslands. Some pit vipers live on the ground, while others live in trees.
Food:	Pit vipers eat mostly rodents and birds. They may also eat lizards, frogs, and other snakes.
Habits:	Pit vipers are sit-and-wait predators. They wait for prey to come near before they strike.
Reproduction:	Most pit vipers are ovoviviparous. Their eggs develop and hatch inside the female's body. She then gives birth to live young. Some pit vipers are oviparous. These females lay eggs that develop and hatch outside their bodies.

CHAPTER 1

Pit Vipers

Pit vipers are named for the heat-sensing pits on their faces. These openings are between the snake's eyes and nostrils. The pits sense an animal's body heat to help the snake find prey.

Viperidae Family

Scientists divide snakes into families. All the snakes in each of these groups have similar features. Pit vipers are members of the Viperidae family. There are more than 220 species in the group.

All snakes in the Viperidae family have hinged fangs. These long, hollow teeth fold up

A pit viper's heat-sensing pits help it find prey.

Pit vipers' fangs move forward and lock into place when the snake is ready to strike.

when the snake's mouth is closed. The fangs lie flat along the roof of the mouth and move forward when the snake is ready to strike. The fangs then lock into place to help catch and kill prey.

Viperidae Subfamilies and Genera

Scientists further divide the snakes of the Viperidae family into subfamilies. Each subfamily is separated based on physical features. All pit vipers have heat-sensing pits. They make up the Crotalinae subfamily.

Pit vipers have another common feature. They are all venomous. They inject venom into prey when they bite. This liquid flows through the snake's hollow fangs and kills prey. The venom can harm large animals and even people.

Scientists also divide snake families and subfamilies into genera. There are 18 genera in the Crotalinae subfamily. Some well-known pit vipers include rattlesnakes, copperheads, cottonmouths, bushmasters, and fer-de-lances.

CHAPTER 2

Pit Viper Species

P it vipers have wide, triangular heads. Venom glands on each side of their heads cause this shape. The glands produce venom.

Copperheads

Copperheads are named for their red-brown color. They can also be gray or pink-brown. These snakes have bands of color on their backs. Each band is an hourglass shape. The snakes can be 2 to 3 feet (60 to 90 centimeters) long.

Pit vipers' venom glands give their heads a triangular shape.

The cottonmouth gets its name from the white lining inside its mouth.

Cottonmouths

When threatened, a cottonmouth stretches its mouth wide open. It shows sharp fangs and the cotton-white colored lining inside its mouth. This display often scares away predators.

Cottonmouths are dark olive or black. Their underbellies are a lighter color. Their color helps them hide in water, where they spend much of their time. The cottonmouth snake is sometimes called a water moccasin. Some cottonmouths grow to 6 feet (1.8 meters) long.

Rattlesnakes

Rattlesnakes earned their name because of the rattles on their tails. The rattle is made up of rings of a hard material called keratin. One ring fits loosely inside the next one. When a snake shakes its tail, the rattle makes a buzzing sound. The sound warns predators of danger.

Most rattlesnakes are red-brown, brown, or gray. Orange, yellow, or white scales form patterns on their backs. Most patterns look like diamonds, spots, or stripes.

Rattlesnakes vary in size. Pygmy rattlesnakes grow to about 2 feet (60 centimeters) long. The eastern diamondback can be up to 8 feet (2.4 meters) long.

Fer-de-Lances

The fer-de-lance snake's head is pointed. It looks like a lance, a spear with a pointed end. Most fer-de-lances are brown, gray, olive, or green. They usually have markings on their bodies that help them hide. Some species of fer-de-lance grow to more than 8 feet (2.4 meters) long.

PIT VIPER SPECIES

common name	scientific name
bushmaster - *Lachesis muta*	
copperhead - *Agkistrodon contortrix*	
cottonmouth - *Agkistrodon piscivorus*	
eyelash viper - *Bothriechis schlegelii*	
fer-de-lance - *Bothrops* genus	
rattlesnakes - *Crotalus* and *Sistrurus* genera	

Some fer-de-lance snakes have powerful venom. Their venom can kill a person in a few hours. Fer-de-lances have killed more people in Central America and South America than any other snake. Most people bitten by these snakes say they never saw the snakes nearby.

Bushmasters

The bushmaster's scientific name means "silent fate." This snake was given the name because it is very shy. These snakes are not

Bushmasters may be hard to find because they blend well with their surroundings.

commonly seen in the wild. Their gray and brown color and large diamond-shaped patterns on their back help them hide.

These snakes are the largest pit vipers in the world. They can grow to 12 feet (3.7 meters) in length. Bushmasters have long fangs and powerful venom. A bite from a bushmaster can kill a person in a few hours.

Head

Heat-Sensing
Pit

Nostril

16

Tail

Copperhead

CHAPTER 3

Habitat

Pit vipers live in many places of the world. Many pit vipers live in North America and South America. These two continents are sometimes referred to as the New World. Pit vipers in these places are often called New World pit vipers. Other pit vipers live in Asia. They are referred to as Old World pit vipers.

Rattlesnakes

Rattlesnakes are New World pit vipers. They range from southern Canada to Argentina. In the United States, they are found in almost every state. Only Alaska, Delaware, Hawaii, and Maine do not have rattlesnakes.

Rattlesnakes live throughout North, Central, and South America.

Rattlesnakes live in different habitats. Some live in mountains or in meadows. Others live in forests or along swamp edges. Many rattlesnakes live in deserts or other dry areas. The largest populations live in the southwestern United States and northwestern Mexico.

Cottonmouths and Copperheads

Cottonmouths and copperheads live mainly in the southeastern United States. They range from southern Illinois to Florida.

Cottonmouths and copperheads can be found in swamps, streams, ditches, and marshes. Cottonmouths spend much of their lives in water.

Fer-de-Lances and Bushmasters

Fer-de-lances live in Central America and South America. They live mostly in forests and along rivers and streams. Fer-de-lances have been known to hunt in fields for rodents. One species, the desert lancehead, lives in the desert of northern Chile.

A fer-de-lance's head is pointed like a lance.

Bushmasters also live in Central and South America. They are found in rain forests and on forested mountains. Some hunt in areas of recently cleared land. Bushmasters often hide in old animal burrows. They also hide among plants and bushes while waiting for prey.

Other Pit Vipers

Many pit vipers live in Asia. Pit vipers in Asia include the Malayan pit viper, the hump-nosed viper, and the hundred-pace snake. They live in forests, hills, and fields. Some pit vipers live in mountains. These snakes include the Himalayan pit viper and the Siberian pit viper.

Not all pit vipers live on the ground. Some species live in trees. The Wagler's pit vipers of Southeast Asia spend most of their lives in trees. Eyelash vipers of Central America also hang from tree branches. Fer-de-lances and Asian pit vipers sometimes climb trees to hunt.

Eyelash vipers spend much of their time in trees. They are named for the scales above their eyes that look like eyelashes.

CHAPTER 4

Hunting

P it vipers eat any animals they can catch and kill. The animals pit vipers eat depend on their habitat. Pit vipers that live in or near water eat fish, frogs, turtles, and lizards. Those in forests eat birds, rodents, and insects.

Sit-and-Wait Predators

Most pit vipers are known as sit-and-wait predators. They wait for prey to come near and then strike.

The snakes' camouflage helps hide them from prey. The Wagler's pit viper is bright green and yellow. It blends in with leaves.

The Wagler's pit viper hunts for prey in trees.

Since this snake spends much of its life in trees, it can be difficult to see.

Most pit vipers are nocturnal. They are active at night. But pit vipers that live in cold areas are active during the day. Once the sun sets, it is too cold for them to move around.

Senses for Hunting

Pit vipers cannot hear sounds as people do. They do not have ears outside their body. Instead, they use their bodies to feel sounds. As prey nears, pit vipers feel the movement in the ground. The snakes can even feel the movements of a mouse.

Many pit vipers can see well at night. During the day, their pupils are small slits. At night, the pupils open wide to let in light. Still, pit vipers cannot see as well as people do. They can see some movement and tell the difference between light and dark.

Pit vipers rely on their sense of smell to hunt. They flick out their tongues to collect scents in the air and on the ground. The tongue carries the scents to the Jacobson's organ. This

A pit viper uses its tongue to find prey.

organ is located on the roof of a snake's mouth. It helps them find and identify prey.

Pit vipers also use their heat-sensing pits to find prey. They can sense a difference in temperature of less than half of a degree. The pits work as long as the prey's body temperature is warmer than the air around it.

Venom

A pit viper strikes as soon as its prey is in reach. The snake's mouth opens wide. The fangs quickly swing forward. As the snake bites into prey, its jaws clamp shut. Venom flows through the fangs and into the prey.

Many pit vipers let go of their prey after they bite it. The bitten animal may try to run away, but the venom affects prey right away. The venom causes the animal's heart and lungs to stop working. The prey usually dies within a few minutes. Pit vipers follow the animal's scent to the place where it dies.

Swallowing Prey

Pit vipers swallow their food whole. Most animals are swallowed headfirst. This is easier for the snakes. It allows the prey's legs to fold up neatly inside the pit viper's body.

A pit viper can swallow prey larger than its mouth. Its upper and lower jaws are connected with ligaments. This stretchy tissue allows the snake to separate its jaws. Strong muscles then help pull the prey from the snake's throat into

Pit vipers swallow prey headfirst.

its stomach. The teeth of a pit viper point backwards to hold the prey in place.

After eating, pit vipers usually rest. Some may wait several weeks or months before eating again. The length of time depends on the size of the prey. If the prey was small, the pit viper will hunt again soon.

CHAPTER 5

Mating

Many pit vipers hibernate in winter. Hibernating pit vipers lie very still. Their breathing and heartbeat slow down. Pit vipers in cold areas may hibernate up to seven months. Snakes that live in warm climates do not hibernate as long.

In spring, the snakes wake up from hibernation. They begin searching for a mate. When females are ready to mate, they give off a scent. Male pit vipers follow the scent to find the females. The scent often attracts more than one male. When this happens, male pit vipers sometimes perform a combat dance.

Pit vipers mate in spring.

Bushmasters hatch from eggs.

Combat Dance

A combat dance is a wrestling match between two male snakes. Each male raises its head and the front half of its body in the air. They wrap their bodies around each other, then try to push each other to the ground. The snakes do not bite during a combat dance. The winner is usually the bigger, stronger male. After the weaker snake is held down, the winner lets the weaker snake leave.

The winning snake then begins courting the female. During courtship, the male rubs his chin along the female's back. He flicks his tongue along her body. Then the two snakes twist together for mating. They may stay joined for several hours.

Birth and Hatching

Many pit vipers are ovoviviparous. Their eggs develop and hatch inside the female's body. The females then give birth to live young. Many pit vipers in cool climates reproduce in this way. The females keep their eggs warm by lying in the sun. The eggs need warmth to develop properly.

A few pit vipers, such as bushmasters, are oviparous. They lay eggs that develop and hatch outside the female's body. The bushmaster is the only New World pit viper that lays eggs. The female places the eggs in

Some young pit vipers attract prey with their yellow-tipped tail.

an old animal burrow. The young hatch 75 to 80 days later. Female bushmasters coil their bodies around the eggs until they hatch to protect the eggs from predators.

The young snakes use an egg tooth to cut an opening in the leathery egg. An egg tooth is a tiny thorn-like spur on a young snake's upper jaw. It falls off soon after hatching.

Young

Most pit vipers are born or hatched in late summer. Two to 80 young can be born at one time. The young can be 7 to 20 inches (18 to 51 centimeters) long, depending on the species. They must care for themselves as soon as they are born or hatched. The young eat insects and small animals.

Pit vipers are venomous the moment they are born. A young pit viper's venom is just as strong as the adults' venom.

Some species of young pit vipers have a yellow tip on their tails. They wiggle their tails to attract prey. Animals may think the yellow tip is a worm. When prey nears, the young pit vipers strike.

CHAPTER 6

Pit Vipers and People

Pit vipers can benefit people. They eat rats and mice. These rodents can eat farmers' crops and spread diseases. Scientists use pit viper venom to make antivenin. People bitten by venomous snakes are treated with this medicine. People who do not get the antivenin can die, depending on the kind of snake that bit them.

Because pit vipers are dangerous, they do not make good pets. Only people who are snake experts should handle them.

People get venom from pit vipers to make antivenin.

A rattlesnake shakes its tail as a warning.

Myths

There are many myths about pit vipers. One myth says that pit vipers always coil their bodies before they strike. Many pit vipers do coil their bodies before striking. But they can bite at any time. Their bodies do not have to be in a certain position. Coiling only gives the snakes more distance to strike.

Another myth says that a rattlesnake's age can be determined by counting the number of rattles on its tail. The truth is that one segment is added each time the snake sheds its skin. Some rattlesnakes shed more than others. Also, the tips of the rattles can break off. Counting the rattles does not tell a snake's age.

One of the biggest myths is that rattlesnakes always shake their tails before striking. But a rattlesnake can strike at any time. The noise its tail makes is a warning that danger is near. It is a way the snake defends itself.

Defenses

Besides rattlesnakes, other pit vipers shake their tails. They do not have rattles, but they can make a similar noise. When threatened, the bushmaster shakes its tail so fast it makes a buzzing noise. The fer-de-lance shakes its tail in a pile of leaves to make the sound. These actions are used to scare away predators.

Pit vipers rely on camouflage to hide from danger. Birds of prey, such as owls and eagles, eat pit vipers.

Most people who are bitten by pit vipers never saw them hiding. They may have accidentally stepped on the snake. Some pit vipers are easily threatened. They may strike just because a person is getting close.

Pit vipers are thought of as dangerous to people because of their venom. But they do not look for people to bite. They only bite when they feel threatened. Still, people should keep their distance when they see a pit viper.

Rattlesnakes can strike very quickly.

Words to Know

antivenin (ant-ee-VEN-in)—a medicine made from snake venom used to treat snake bites

burrow (BUR-oh)—a hole in the ground often made by an animal

camouflage (KAM-uh-flahzh)—coloring that makes animals look like their surroundings

carnivore (KAR-nuh-vor)—an animal that hunts and eats other animals

genus (JEE-nuss)—a group of plants or animals that are related; genera is more than one genus.

gland (GLAND)—an organ in the body that makes natural substances; a pit viper has two venom glands in its head.

hibernate (HYE-bur-nate)—to be inactive during the winter

lance (LANSS)—a spear with a pointed end

nocturnal (nahk-TUR-nuhl)—active at night

oviparous (oh-VIP-uh-rus)—laying eggs that develop and hatch outside the female's body

ovoviviparous (oh-voh-vye-VIP-uh-rus)—having eggs that develop and hatch inside the female's body; ovoviviparous animals give birth to live young.

predator (PRED-uh-tur)—an animal that hunts other animals for food

prey (PRAY)—an animal hunted by another animal for food

pupil (PYOO-puhl)—the round, black center of the eye that lets in light

species (SPEE-sheez)—a specific type of plant or animal

venom (VEN-uhm)—a poisonous liquid produced by some snakes, such as pit vipers

Cottonmouth

To Learn More

Arnosky, Jim. *All About Rattlesnakes*. New York: Scholastic, 2002.

George, Linda. *Cottonmouths*. Snakes. Mankato, Minn.: Capstone Press, 1998.

Jackson, Tom. *Rattlesnakes*. Nature's Children. Danbury, Conn.: Grolier Educational, 2001.

Mattison, Christopher. *Snake*. New York: DK Publishing, 1999.

Robinson, Claire. *Snakes*. Heinemann First Library in the Wild. Des Plaines, Ill.: Heinemann Library, 1999.

Useful Addresses

Arizona Herpetological Association
P.O. Box 64531
Phoenix, AZ 85082-4531

Black Hills Reptile Gardens
P.O. Box 620
Rapid City, SD 57709

New England Herpetological Society
P.O. Box 1082
Boston, MA 02103

The Ontario Herpetological Society
P.O. Box 244
Stn Port Credit
Mississauga, ON L5G 4L8
Canada

Internet Sites

Do you want to learn more about pit vipers and other snakes?
Visit the FactHound at *http://www.facthound.com*

FactHound can track down many sites to help you. All the FactHound sites are hand-selected by our editors. FactHound will fetch the best, most accurate information to answer your questions.

IT'S EASY! IT'S FUN!
1) Go to *http://www.facthound.com*
2) Type in: 0736821384
3) Click on "FETCH IT" and FactHound will put you on the trail of several helpful links.

You can also search by subject or book title. So, relax and let our pal FactHound do the research for you!

Index